THE BRITISH MUSEUM
Timeline of the Ancient World

Mesopotamia ■ Egypt
Greece ■ Rome

Katharine Wiltshire

THE BRITISH MUSEUM PRESS

© 2004 The Trustees of the British Museum

Published in 2004 by British Museum Press
A division of British Museum Company Ltd
46 Bloomsbury Street, London WC1B 3QQ

ISBN 0 7141 3029 X

Katharine Wiltshire has asserted the right to be identified
as the author of this work.

A catalogue record for this title is available from the
British Library.

Designed and typeset by Peter Bailey for Proof Books

Printed and bound by Hung Hing Co Ltd, China

Illustration Acknowledgements

All photographs are © The Trustees of the British Museum,
taken by the British Museum Photography and Imaging
Department, unless otherwise stated.

Maps by ML Design.

pp. 4 top left Photograph © 2003 Museum of Fine Arts,
Boston. King Menkaure (Mycerinus) and Queen. Egyptian,
Old Kingdom, Dynasty 4, reign of Menkaure, about 2490-
2472 B.C. Findspot: Egypt. Giza, Menkaure Valley Temple.
Greywacke. Height x width x depth: 142.2 x 57.1 x 55.2
cm. Harvard University – Museum of Fine Arts Expedition.
11.1738

p. 4 bottom right Peter Clayton.

p. 6 centre left copyright Steve Day.

p. 7 bottom left, p. 29 bottom (and timeline) Robert
Harding Picture Library.

p. 11 centre left (and timeline) The Bridgeman Art Library.

p. 12 top left Astrid & Hanns-Frieder Michler/Science Photo
Library.

p. 13 bottom left (and timeline) and p. 13 bottom right
Robert Harding Picture Library.

p. 14 bottom left Werner Forman Archive/Egyptian
Museum, Cairo.

p. 15 bottom left (and p. 1 and timeline) © Bildarchiv
Preussischer Kulturbesitz, Berlin/Agyptisches Museum,
Berlin.

p. 17 centre right (and timeline) Robert Harding Picture
Library.

p. 17 centre left and p. 17 bottom Richard Parkinson.

p.18 bottom left (and timeline), p. 18 top right (and
timeline) and p. 18 bottom centre Robert Harding Picture
Library.

p.19 bottom right Graham Harrison.

p. 21 bottom left (and p. 1 and timeline) The Bridgeman Art
Library/Giraudon.

p. 21 bottom right The Lesley and Roy Adkins Picture
Library.

p. 23 top left Sonia Halliday Picture Library/photograph:
FHC Birch.

p. 23 centre (and timeline) Peter Clayton.

p. 23 bottom (and timeline) Robert Harding Picture Library.

p. 24 centre right Richard Woff.

p. 25 bottom left Robert Harding Picture Library.

p. 26 top left (and timeline) Peter Clayton.

p. 27 bottom right (and timeline) Hadrian's Wall Tourism
partnership, photo: Graeme Peacock.

p. 28 top left Napoli, Museo Nazionale © 2003, Foto Scala,
Firenze.

p. 29 top right (and timeline) and p. 29 centre left The
Lesley and Roy Adkins Picture Library.

p. 29 centre right Peter Clayton.

p. 30 top left (and timeline) The Lesley and Roy Adkins
Picture Library.

p. 30 bottom right (and timeline) Peter Clayton.

p. 31 centre right Peter Clayton.

p. 31 bottom right Robert Harding Picture Library.

Timeline 1400 BC Akhenaten and Nefertiti: © Bildarchiv
Preussischer Kulturbesitz, Berlin/Agyptisches Museum,
Berlin.

CONTENTS

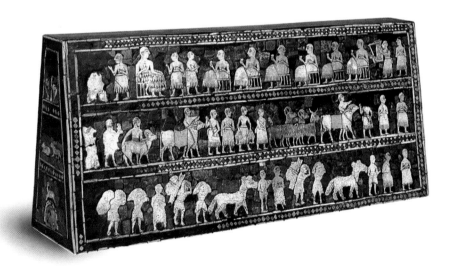

INTRODUCTION TO THE ANCIENT WORLD

IN ANCIENT TIMES, there were many different groups of people living across the world. Gradually, some early nomadic people settled down to become farmers and they began to live in villages and towns. In time, some of these people were able to produce enough surplus food to support specialized workers such as scribes, religious leaders and craftworkers. In addition, they often traded with faraway places, used writing to record activities, information and ideas, built large public, royal and religious buildings, had an organized form of government and produced monumental artworks. When all these things happen in one place, it is known as a civilization.

In this book, we will look at the great civilizations of Mesopotamia, ancient Egypt, ancient Greece and Rome. These four civilizations were very important in the ancient world and in many ways we still feel their influence today. Their stories will take us in time from prehistory (the earliest times) through to the division of the Roman empire in AD 395.

Other ancient civilizations also flourished during this period. In the Indus valley in northern India, a civilization emerged which was to last for over three thousand years; ancient China was ruled by successive powerful dynasties of emperors; and in Central America the Maya civilization built huge monumental structures and produced elaborate stone artwork. You will find information about some of these civilizations in the world section of the timeline.

ABOVE *Statue of the ancient Egyptian king Menkaure II and queen Khamerernebty. Menkaure ruled Egypt during the period of Egyptian history known as the Old Kingdom. Both he and the queen were buried in pyramids at Giza.*

ABOVE *Some of the earliest Mesopotamian literature includes stories about gods and goddesses. This cylinder seal and its impression show a scene from the story of the Zu bird and Ea, the god of water and wisdom.*

ABOVE *When the western Roman empire ended, the Italian peninsula divided into many small kingdoms, each with its own king. This ring, which dates from the 6th century AD, possibly belonged to a royal official who worked for a king in either the Lombard or Ostrogoth kingdom.*

RIGHT *These dolphins are part of the wall decoration in a palace on the island of Crete. Different cultures emerged at different times in Greek history. One of the first cultures developed on the island of Crete. It was followed by the Mycenaean culture on the Greek mainland and then the rise to power of different city states, such as Sparta and Corinth.*

HOW TO USE THIS BOOK

THIS BOOK PROVIDES information on four ancient civilizations – Mesopotamia, Egypt, Greece and Rome. Each part begins with an introduction which provides a general overview of the civilization. It is followed by sections on rulers, writing, learning and buildings. After these, you will find further information on events, activities or places specific to each civilization, such as the ancient Greek Olympic Games or mummification in ancient Egypt.

You can use each part to explore one of the civilizations in depth. Or, you can follow a theme across all four parts by comparing, for example, writing in Mesopotamia, ancient Egypt, ancient Greece and Rome. This will enable you to explore the similarities and differences between the four civilizations by comparing how they were ruled, how they used writing to record things, how they developed new ideas and learning, and how they constructed buildings.

Many of the dates referred to in the book are also shown on the timeline. Remember that the further back in time we look, the more difficult it is to be precise about exactly when things happened. People in the past did not always write down the dates of events. Also, as historians and archaeologists gather new information, dates may change. So you may find different dates in other books for some of the events mentioned in this timeline.

ABOVE *Augustus was the first emperor of Rome. His reign marks the beginning of what is known today as the Imperial Period of Roman history, when the Roman empire was ruled by emperors.*

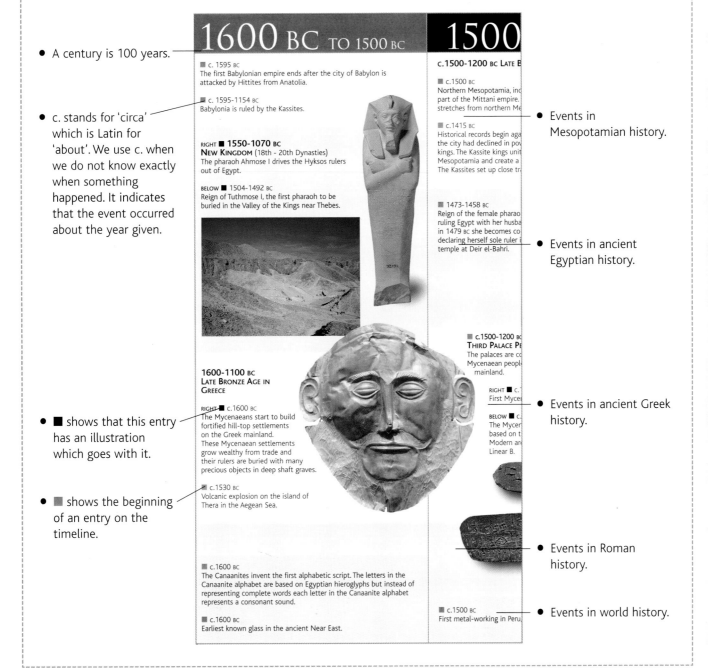

- A century is 100 years.

- c. stands for 'circa' which is Latin for 'about'. We use c. when we do not know exactly when something happened. It indicates that the event occurred about the year given.

- ■ shows that this entry has an illustration which goes with it.

- ■ shows the beginning of an entry on the timeline.

1600 BC TO 1500 BC · 1500

■ c. 1595 BC
The first Babylonian empire ends after the city of Babylon is attacked by Hittites from Anatolia.

■ c. 1595-1154 BC
Babylonia is ruled by the Kassites.

RIGHT ■ **1550-1070 BC**
NEW KINGDOM (18th - 20th Dynasties)
The pharaoh Ahmose I drives the Hyksos rulers out of Egypt.

BELOW ■ 1504-1492 BC
Reign of Tuthmose I, the first pharaoh to be buried in the Valley of the Kings near Thebes.

1600-1100 BC
LATE BRONZE AGE IN GREECE

RIGHT ■ c.1600 BC
The Mycenaeans start to build fortified hill-top settlements on the Greek mainland. These Mycenaean settlements grow wealthy from trade and their rulers are buried with many precious objects in deep shaft graves.

☑ c.1530 BC
Volcanic explosion on the island of Thera in the Aegean Sea.

■ c.1600 BC
The Canaanites invent the first alphabetic script. The letters in the Canaanite alphabet are based on Egyptian hieroglyphs but instead of representing complete words each letter in the Canaanite alphabet represents a consonant sound.

■ c.1600 BC
Earliest known glass in the ancient Near East.

c.1500-1200 BC LATE B

■ c.1500 BC
Northern Mesopotamia, inc part of the Mittani empire. stretches from northern Me

■ c.1415 BC
Historical records begin aga the city had declined in pov kings. The Kassite kings unit Mesopotamia and create a The Kassites set up close tr

■ 1473-1458 BC
Reign of the female pharao ruling Egypt with her husba in 1479 BC she becomes co declaring herself sole ruler i temple at Deir el-Bahri.

■ c.1500-1200 BC
THIRD PALACE PE
The palaces are co Mycenaean peopl mainland.

RIGHT ■ c.
First Myce

BELOW ■ c.
The Myce based on t Modern ar Linear B.

■ c.1500 BC
First metal-working in Peru.

- Events in Mesopotamian history.

- Events in ancient Egyptian history.

- Events in ancient Greek history.

- Events in Roman history.

- Events in world history.

MEASURING TIME

ABOVE *The Romans named the month of August after the emperor Augustus. The month of July was named after Julius Caesar.*

PEOPLE HAVE USED many ways of measuring time. Early people probably observed changes in the natural environment. The different seasons (winter, spring, summer, autumn) showed that time was passing. The movement of the sun and moon in the sky might also have been used to measure time.

In Britain, early people probably used Stonehenge to mark time, based on the position of the sun over particular stones at different times of the year. People also divided time into shorter periods. In Mesopotamia, the Sumerians used a mathematical system based on the number 60. This meant that they divided an hour of time into 60 minutes. We still do this today. The Sumerian calendar was based on the movement of the moon in the night sky. This sort of calendar is called a lunar calendar. Babylonian astronomers observed and recorded the movement of the sun and moon. They used this information to predict when events, such as solar eclipses, were going to happen.

The ancient Egyptians numbered each year of a pharaoh's reign. So they said that an event happened, for example, in the sixth or tenth or twenty-third year of a particular pharaoh's reign. This Egyptian calendar had 365 days in each year. The ancient Egyptians also used two other calendars based on the sun and the moon. Their year started on the autumn equinox (23 September), when day and night are the same length. The ancient Greek year started at the winter solstice (21 December), which is the shortest day of the year.

The earliest Roman calendar consisted of 10 months and had 304 days. Later, two extra months were added, making a calendar of 12 months with 355 days. Then, on 1 January, 45 BC, the Roman ruler Julius Caesar introduced the Julian calendar. Under this calendar, each year had 365 days with an extra day in February every fourth year. Each year was divided into twelve months which were named after Roman rulers, gods and numbers. The Gregorian calendar used in many countries nowadays is based on this Roman calendar.

ABOVE *Every four years, the people of Athens held the Great Panathenaic Festival. This section of frieze from the Parthenon shows the sacred robe which was carried in a procession though the city's streets and dedicated to the goddess Athena on the city's Acropolis.*

LEFT *Stonehenge is made of several circles of stones. The stones were put up at different times over a period of several thousand years. Some of the stones line up with the position of the sun in the sky at different times of the year.*

RIGHT *Over time, the ancient Egyptians developed several different forms of writing. Two of these scripts have been used on this piece of papyrus. Hieroglyphic script is above the picture, while the rest of the text is written in a quicker form of hieroglyphs known as hieratic. The ancient Egyptians later developed a third form of hieroglyphs known as Demotic.*

DATES

THE DATES USED in this book, and on the accompanying timeline, are based on a system where years are numbered backwards and forwards from the year 1. It is a system developed by the Christian faith. Year 1 is the traditional date when Jesus Christ was born. The years before Christ was born are numbered backwards in time and the numbers for these years are followed by the letters BC, which stands for 'Before Christ'. So the year 100 BC is earlier than the year 50 BC. The numbers for the years after Christ's birth have the letters AD before them. The letters AD stand for the Latin phrase 'Anno Domini', which means 'In the year of our Lord'. So the year AD 50 is earlier than the year AD 100.

ABOVE *This Roman mosaic may be the earliest known portrait of Christ.*

Sometimes we do not know exactly when an event happened. In this case, we use 'c.' (short for the Latin word 'circa') before the date. Circa means 'about'. It shows that an event happened around the year given.

In some books, you will see that instead of BC the letters BCE are used. BCE stands for 'Before the common era' and is another way of referring to the years before the traditional birth year of Jesus Christ, but without using his name. The letters AD are replaced by the letters CE, which stand for 'Common era' and refer to the years after the year AD 1.

This system is only one way of dividing up the thousands of years of human history. Jewish people believe that the Torah, the Jewish sacred book, tells them when God created the world. They use this date to start numbering the following years. In the Jewish system, the year AD 2000 would be the year 5761. Jewish months start at the new moon and last 29 or 30 days. There is an extra month every three years to keep the months in line with the seasons.

The Muslim system of numbering years starts with the year in which the prophet Muhammad moved from Mecca to Medinah. In the Muslim system, the year AD 2000 would be the Muslim year 1422 AH. AH stands for the Latin phrase 'Anno Hegirae', which means 'The years after the emigration [to Medinah]'. Muslims use a lunar calendar. There are 12 months in the Muslim year. Each month starts at the new moon.

ABOVE *This list of kings' names was carved on a wall at the temple of Abydos in Egypt. Ancient Egyptians numbered years from the beginning of each king's reign.*

RIGHT AND ABOVE *This Roman coin, issued in AD 80, commemorates the building of the Colosseum in Rome (shown above).*

MESOPOTAMIA

MESOPOTAMIA IS THE AREA of land between the River Euphrates and the River Tigris. In ancient times, both rivers frequently flooded the surrounding land. Each time the floodwater went down, it left behind a layer of silt, creating a fertile area of soil near the rivers. The first people to live in Mesopotamia led a nomadic life. Then around 6000 BC people began to keep animals and grow their own food crops on the fertile river soil in northern Mesopotamia. In the south, where there was less natural rainfall, they built canals to bring water from the river to water the fields. These first farmers settled in one place and lived in small villages. Some of these villages grew into towns, and in turn some of the towns grew into cities. The cities became wealthy from agriculture and trade. Across Mesopotamia, different groups of people emerged, based around particular cities. The Sumerians were to be found in southern Mesopotamia, the Akkadians, and then the Babylonians, in central Mesopotamia, and the Assyrians in northern Mesopotamia. Sometimes, the whole of Mesopotamia was ruled by one of these groups. Sometimes, it was conquered and ruled by people who came from outside Mesopotamia.

ABOVE *King Hammurabi was the ruler of Babylon from 1792 to 1750 BC. In the 29th year of his reign, he took control of many other cities in southern Mesopotamia and created the first Babylonian empire.*

LEFT *This glazed jar comes from Assyria. It is decorated with a pattern of leaf shapes. Coloured glazes were also used in Mesopotamia to decorate building bricks.*

ABOVE *Map of ancient Mesopotamia.*

RIGHT *There were no metal mines in Mesopotamia. The silver to make this jug was imported by Sumerian traders. The Sumerians were skilled metalworkers.*

RIGHT *This small limestone statue shows a woman worshipping one of the Sumerian gods. The Sumerians were the first people to live in cities in southern Mesopotamia.*

RULERS

THE EARLY CITIES in Mesopotamia were city-states. Each city was governed by its own ruler and surrounded by farmland which provided food for the people who lived in the city. Sometimes, one of these cities would become particularly powerful and would rule the other cities around it. Sometimes, such a city was powerful enough to rule all of Mesopotamia. From about 3000 BC, the Sumerians built a number of powerful city-states across southern Mesopotamia. At the same time, the Akkadians were settling and building cities in central Mesopotamia. One of the Akkadian kings, king Sargon (who reigned from c. 2334 to 2279 BC), also took control of Sumer and ruled Mesopotamia as a single country.

Mesopotamia was ruled by the Akkadians until c. 2193 BC, when the Sumerian cities went back to being ruled by individual rulers. Around 2110 BC, king Ur-Nammu of Ur (who reigned from c. 2112 to 2095 BC) reunited the Sumerian cities. His son Shulgi (who reigned from c. 2095 to 2047 BC) created an empire which controlled the whole of Mesopotamia. However, other cities and people were growing powerful. During the early 1700s BC, king Hammurabi of Babylon (who reigned from c.1792 to 1750 BC) founded the Babylonian empire, which included the whole of southern Mesopotamia together with the area of northern Mesopotamia which had been controlled by the Assyrians. In 1595 BC, the Hittites, from what is now central Turkey, captured Babylon. Later, the city and southern Mesopotamia were ruled by the Kassite kings. In the north, the Assyrian kingdom, with its main city at Ashur in the valley of the River Tigris, grew increasingly important. During the 9th century BC, the Assyrian kings moved their capital to Kalhu (now known as Nimrud), began to expand their kingdom and gradually took control of all of Mesopotamia. By 650 BC, under the rule of king Ashurbanipal, and with Nineveh as the capital city, the Assyrian empire was at its greatest extent, stretching from Mesopotamia across to the Mediterranean Sea and Egypt. However, in 612 BC, the Babylonians and Medes revolted against Assyrian rule and attacked all the major Assyrian cities. Mesopotamia was then controlled by the neo-Babylonian empire founded in 625 BC.

ABOVE *This stone stela shows the Assyrian king Ashurnasirpal II, who reigned from 883 to 859 BC. The writing on the stela includes a description of the building of the city of Kalhu (Nimrud), which took place during Ashurnasirpal's reign.*

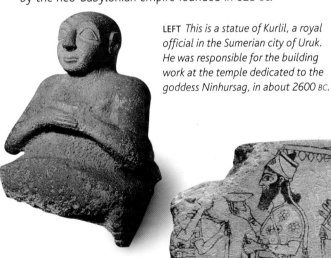

LEFT *This is a statue of Kurlil, a royal official in the Sumerian city of Uruk. He was responsible for the building work at the temple dedicated to the goddess Ninhursag, in about 2600 BC.*

ABOVE *This statue of a Babylonian woman probably comes from a temple. Babylonian queens often controlled their own royal lands, had their own royal officials, and were actively involved in the economy of their region.*

RIGHT *This glazed tile comes from a royal palace at Kalhu (Nimrud). It shows an Assyrian king with his attendants.*

ABOVE *A teacher wrote some cuneiform words on one side of this clay tablet and then the pupil practised the same words on the other side.*

■ WRITING

WRITING BEGAN in the Sumerian cities around 3200 BC. Writing was used to record the collection and distribution of food. The first Sumerian writing used pictograms. Pictograms are simple pictures which represent objects. Gradually, these pictograms changed into a form of writing which used wedge-shapes. We call this writing cuneiform. Cuneiform symbols represented syllables which could be combined to make a word, or used by themselves to represent a complete word, an object or an idea. Eventually, there were more than 600 cuneiform symbols. The first cuneiform represented the Sumerian language. Later, the Assyrians and Babylonians also wrote their languages down using cuneiform.

Most of the writing from Mesopotamia is on small clay tablets. Damp clay was formed into a flat tablet, which could be held in one hand. The writer pressed a stylus made from reed, wood or ivory into the clay to make the cuneiform symbols, then left the tablet in the sun to harden. From about 1300 BC, wooden or ivory tablets covered with a layer of wax were also used for writing. These could be reused, since the wax could be smoothed over ready for the next piece of writing. Cuneiform signs were also carved onto stone.

It took a long time to learn to read and to write cuneiform with over 600 signs to remember. Scribes learnt cuneiform at an *edubba*, which means 'tablet house'. Cuneiform was used in Mesopotamia for over 3000 years. Its last known use is a second-century AD Babylonian astronomy text.

ABOVE *This stone stela, covered in cuneiform writing, was set up in memory of a priest called Adad-etir by his son.*

ABOVE *The pictogram on this stone tablet probably records the sale of a piece of land, with pictures of the people buying and selling. The tablet also says how much the land cost.*

RIGHT *The writer of this letter ran out of space, and had to continue on a separate small tablet. Both tablets were then put into the clay envelope shown on the left.*

■ LEARNING

ABOVE *A clay mask of the legendary giant Humbaba, who was one of the characters in the Epic of Gilgamesh.*

MESOPOTAMIAN CITIES were centres of knowledge and learning. The Sumerians developed a number system based on 60. The Assyrians occasionally used a system based on 10. To help with mathematical calculations, people used multiplication tables written on clay tablets. Babylonian astronomers studied the night sky and recorded the movement of the moon and planets. The Sumerians started to write down stories about their kings and gods from about 2500 BC. Cuneiform tablets containing stories, histories and scientific information were kept in the royal palaces and temples. The Assyrian king Ashurbanipal (who reigned from 668 to 631 BC) collected a library of about 25,000 clay tablets at his palace at Nineveh. The tablets included letters, legends, dictionaries and histories, mathematical and medical texts. The Babylonian king Nebuchadnezzar II (who reigned from 605 to 562 BC) started a museum in Babylon, which contained objects, statues and clay tablets, some of which dated back to Sumerian times.

ABOVE *This clay tablet from king Ashurbanipal's library includes part of the Epic of Gilgamesh. The story started as a collection of oral stories which was later written down.*

RIGHT *A Babylonian map of the world, made around 550 BC. The city of Babylon is marked in the centre with all the known lands around it. The circle around the edge is the sea. The vertical lines are probably the River Euphrates.*

■ BUILDINGS

MOST MESOPOTAMIAN buildings were built using timber and mud bricks. These bricks were made from river mud, which was shaped and then dried in the sun. The mud-brick walls were plastered and whitewashed.

Some houses in the cities were two stories high and built facing into a central courtyard. A city also contained the royal palace, temples, workshops, shops and schools. High walls were built around the cities to protect them from floods and attack. The most important buildings in a city, such as the royal palace, were decorated with sculptures, and the walls were probably painted. Many Assyrian kings decorated their palaces with carved stone wall reliefs.

The city of Babylon was the capital city for the Babylonian empire. It was rebuilt under the Babylonian king Nebuchadnezzar II (who reigned from 605 to 562 BC) with massive surrounding walls, strong gates and a seven-storey ziggurat. The royal palace was so grand that Nebuchadnezzar called it 'the marvel of all people, the centre of the land, the shining residence, the dwelling of majesty'. He also built the Hanging Gardens of Babylon. This was a terraced garden full of trees and flowering plants, built to remind his wife, queen Amytis, of the green hills of her home land in Media.

ABOVE *A carved stone relief from the walls of the North Palace at Nineveh. It shows the Assyrian king Ashurbanipal and queen Ashur-sharratt sitting in a garden.*

ABOVE *The city of Babylon was surrounded by high walls and great gateways. Each gate was dedicated to a god. This is a modern (half-size) reconstruction of the gate of the goddess Ishtar. It was decorated with colourful glazed bricks showing bulls and dragons.*

ABOVE *A cylinder seal and impression of the goddess Ishtar. She is the tall figure at the right-hand end.*

ABOVE *This stone statue of a human-headed winged bull is over 3 metres (10 ft) tall. It stood at one of the entrances to an inner courtyard of the North-West Palace at Kalhu (Nimrud). The statue has five legs, because it was designed to be looked at either from the front or from the side.*

11

POTAMIA

ABOVE *The early farmers used the seeds from wild plants to start to grow their own cereal crops.*

ABOVE *Early farmers kept herds of sheep.*

EARLY FARMING

THE FIRST FARMERS settled in Mesopotamia around 6000 BC. At first, they lived in northern Mesopotamia where there was fertile soil and natural rainfall to water their crops. These early farmers grew wild cereal plants and kept sheep and goats. Around 5500 BC, irrigation was developed. This meant river water was carried in canals and ditches to water the soil in regions where there was not much rain. Farmers were now able to settle in central and southern Mesopotamia where there was little natural rainfall. They built earth banks and dug ditches to channel water from the rivers to the fields in which they were growing their crops. Many farming villages grew up near the River Euphrates on the fertile alluvial soil left after the river flooded. Sumerian farmers used a plough which was pulled by oxen. This type of plough was more efficient than a hand-held plough.

ABOVE *This clay tablet is a record of food supplies. The pictograms record different types of food, such as bread, and the circular and curved holes stand for numbers.*

ABOVE *Cows were one of the first wild animals to be domesticated by early farmers. On this frieze, people are milking cows and making butter from the milk.*

FIRST CITIES

THE EARLY FARMING villages were so productive that, as some of the villages grew into towns, many people were able to live in the town without having to farm themselves. This meant that some people were able to work full time as scribes, metalworkers, potters, weavers or bakers. Some towns were able to develop into cities surrounded by farmland which provided enough food for all the people living there. Sumer's first city was Uruk, which was built alongside the River Euphrates. The city was a major religious centre and contained two temples, one dedicated to the god An and the other to the goddess Inanna. By 3400 BC nearly 10,000 people lived in Uruk.

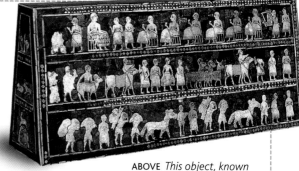

ABOVE *This object, known as the Standard of Ur, was found in the royal cemetery at Ur. This side shows people feasting and listening to music. It is made from white shell, red limestone and blue lapis lazuli. The lapis lazuli came from distant Afghanistan.*

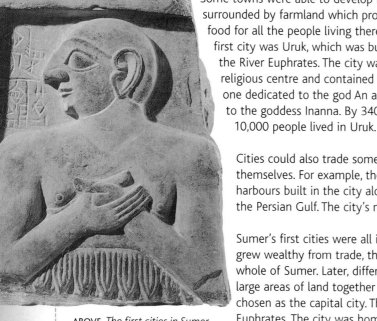

ABOVE *The first cities in Sumer each had their own ruler. This is Enannatum, ruler of the city of Lagash around 2450 BC.*

Cities could also trade some of their produce for goods which they could not grow or make themselves. For example, the city of Ur was Mesopotamia's main port. There were two harbours built in the city alongside the River Euphrates. Ships could sail down the river to the Persian Gulf. The city's merchants traded as far away as India.

Sumer's first cities were all independent, each with its own ruler. However, as the cities grew wealthy from trade, they started to compete with each other for control over the whole of Sumer. Later, different peoples created empires in Mesopotamia which controlled large areas of land together with the cities. Within these empires, particular cities would be chosen as the capital city. The city of Babylon was built on the banks of the River Euphrates. The city was home to the Babylonian king as well as being the commercial, political and religious centre for the Babylonian empire. The first capital city of the Assyrian people was at Ashur on the River Tigris. Later, the capital moved to Kalhu (now known as Nimrud) and then to Nineveh.

ABOVE *Ziggurats were temples for the Mesopotamian gods. Each city built temples to their own favourite gods. This cylinder seal and impression show some of the Mesopotamian gods and goddesses, including Ea, Usimu, Ishtar and Shamash.*

■ ZIGGURATS

SOME ANCIENT MESOPOTAMIAN temples were built on top of tall, stepped structures known as ziggurats. The remains of 19 ziggurats have so far been identified in Mesopotamia. Ziggurats were built in layers of mud bricks, which rose up in square or rectangular platforms to the sacred shrine at the top. Each platform was smaller than the one below and long ramps or flights of stairs were used to climb up from one platform to the next.

The first ziggurats were built by King Ur-Nammu (who reigned from c. 2112 to 2095 BC) in the Sumerian cities of Ur, Eridu, Nippur and Uruk. The ziggurat at Ur was dedicated to the moon god Nanna and a shrine for the god was built at the top. A ziggurat dedicated to the Mesopotamian god Marduk may have been built at Babylon about 1750 BC. By the time of king Nebuchadnezzar II (who reigned from 605 to 562 BC) it had eight platforms of bricks with a temple for Marduk on the summit, where the Babylonians believed the god slept at night. The ziggurat was so tall that it had benches halfway up for people to rest on during the climb up the ramps linking the different platforms. The ziggurat at Dur-Sharrukin, built by the Assyrians c. 710 BC, possibly had a spiral ramp leading to the top, with each platform of bricks painted a different colour.

Religious rituals were performed by priests and priestesses at the top of a ziggurat in honour of the god. The ziggurat was surrounded by a sacred area and a pathway led to the royal palace for ceremonial processions between the two buildings.

ABOVE *This ziggurat at Ur was dedicated to the moon god Nanna in about 2100 BC. It originally had three stages. This is a modern reconstruction of the first stage.*

■ LATER HISTORY

THE NEO-BABYLONIAN empire fell to the Persians in 539 BC, when the Persian king Cyrus entered Babylon and made Mesopotamia part of the Achaemenid Persian empire. The Persian empire was later conquered by the Macedonian ruler Alexander, who made Mesopotamia part of his empire. After Alexander's death in 323 BC, his empire was divided up and Mesopotamia was ruled by the Seleucid dynasty founded by Seleucus, one of Alexander's generals. Then, in 141 BC, the Parthian king Mithradates I took control of Mesopotamia. The Parthians briefly lost control of Mesopotamia when it was invaded by the Romans in AD 115 but it was returned to the Parthians by the Roman emperor Hadrian in AD 117.

ABOVE *By the end of the second century BC, Mesopotamia was part of the Parthian empire. This silver coin shows the Parthian king Mithradates I (reigned 171–138 BC).*

The Parthian empire was overthrown by the Sasanian king Ardashir in AD 224–26. Mesopotamia was then ruled by Sasanian kings until AD 637, when Muslim Arabs invaded the Sasanian empire and Mesopotamia became part of the Islamic empire. From AD 1534 until 1918, Mesopotamia was part of the Turkish empire ruled by the Ottoman dynasty. Today, most of Mesopotamia is the country of Iraq with its capital city at Baghdad, in central Mesopotamia.

RIGHT *The Sasanian empire stretched east of the River Euphrates across into central Asia. This bronze figure shows one of the Sasanian kings.*

ABOVE *Baghdad, the capital city of modern Iraq. The city was founded in AD 762 on the banks of the River Tigris.*

EGYPT

THE RIVER NILE flows through Egypt, bringing water and fertile soil to a desert landscape. People began to farm in the Nile Valley about 6000 BC, using the soil created by the annual flooding of the River Nile. By 4000 BC, sailing boats were being used on the Nile and, by 3500 BC, the first towns were developing from the early farming villages.

At this time, Egypt was ruled by two local rulers – one in Lower Egypt (the land around the Nile Delta) and one in Upper Egypt (the land on either side of the Nile south of the Delta). Around 3100 BC, Egypt was united under one ruler. Narmer was the first king of all Egypt. Kings continued to rule a united Egypt throughout what is known as the Old Kingdom (2686 to 2181 BC). After this, control of Egypt was divided between several local rulers and it was not until 2055 BC that Egypt was reunified by the pharaoh Mentuhotep II. This was the beginning of the Middle Kingdom which lasted until 1650 BC. From 1650 to 1550 BC, Egypt was ruled by Hyksos rulers from Palestine and numerous pharaohs from the city of Thebes. In 1550 BC, the pharaoh Ahmose reunited all of Egypt. This was the start of the New Kingdom which continued until 1069 BC. After 1069 BC, Egypt was ruled by pharaohs who came not only from Egypt but other lands such as Nubia, Persia and Greece. In 30 BC, Egypt became part of the Roman empire ruled by the Roman emperor.

ABOVE *The River Nile was very important to the ancient Egyptians. The annual flood brought fertile soil in which they grew their food crops. The river was also used to transport people and goods up and down the river and out to the Mediterranean Sea.*

LEFT *This slate palette shows Narmer, the first king of all Egypt. On this side Narmer is wearing the white crown of Upper Egypt. The other side shows him wearing the Red Crown of Lower Egypt.*

Egypt

Mediterranean Sea

Alexandria
NILE DELTA
LOWER EGYPT
Giza · Cairo
Saqqara · Memphis

Akhetaten (el-Amarna)

River Nile

UPPER EGYPT

Valley of the Kings
Valley of the Queens · Thebes

NUBIA

100 miles
200 kilometres
Abu Simbel·

ABOVE *Map of ancient Egypt.*

LEFT *This pot was made c.3500 BC. This period of Egyptian history is known as the Predynastic period. The pot is made of clay from the Egyptian desert and is decorated with a picture of a boat.*

ABOVE *A seated statue of the pharaoh Amenhotep III. Papyrus and lotus plants are carved on each side of his throne. These plants are the symbols of Upper and Lower Egypt and show that the pharaoh rules over both lands.*

ABOVE *This tomb painting shows Nebamun, his wife, Hatshepsut, and their daughter. Nebamun was a government scribe. He was in charge of the collection of grain from the farmland around the city of Thebes.*

RULERS

BEFORE 3100 BC, Egypt was controlled by several local rulers. Narmer was the first ruler to unite Egypt as one country, and he became the first king in about 3100 BC. For the next 3000 years, Egypt was ruled by the pharaohs. During the Old, Middle and New Kingdoms, there was a series of strong rulers governing all of Egypt. In between were periods when there were many local rulers or rulers from other lands who took control of Egypt. The ancient Egyptians believed that the pharaoh was a living god. The pharaoh had total authority and was in charge of the army, the treasury and justice in Egypt. To help the pharaoh rule, there were many government officials and scribes. They were in charge of activities such as the irrigation of the fields, grain collection and storage, collecting taxes and keeping written financial and business records. The pharaoh was advised by the vizier (prime minister). Ancient Egypt was divided into districts, called nomes, each with its own set of government officials and scribes. When Egypt became part of the Roman empire in 30 BC, the Roman emperor appointed a Roman governor to be in charge of the Roman province of Egypt.

RIGHT *Queen Nefertiti was the wife of the pharaoh Akhenaten. This portrait of her was found in a sculptor's workshop at Akhetaten.*

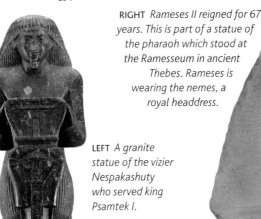

LEFT *A granite statue of the vizier Nespakashuty who served king Psamtek I.*

RIGHT *Rameses II reigned for 67 years. This is part of a statue of the pharaoh which stood at the Ramesseum in ancient Thebes. Rameses is wearing the nemes, a royal headdress.*

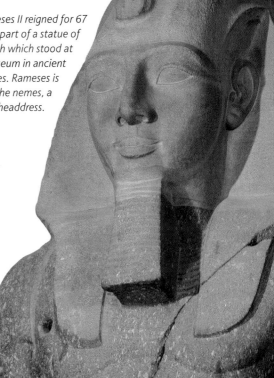

WRITING

FOR OVER 3000 YEARS, the ancient Egyptians used a form of picture-writing, called hieroglyphs. Hieroglyphs could be carved in stone, painted on walls and coffins, or written in ink on papyrus. The hieroglyphic script consisted of about 700 different signs. Over time more signs were added and by around 300 BC there were up to 8000 hieroglyphic signs. Each sign represented a word or a sound. The signs could be put together to make sentences. Hieroglyphs could be written from right to left, left to right or top to bottom. From about 2200 BC, the Egyptians started to use a simplified form of hieroglyphs for writing business contracts, letters, stories and poems. This writing was called hieratic and was much quicker to write than hieroglyphs. Later on, an even faster way of writing hieroglyphic signs was developed, called Demotic.

Ancient Egyptians wrote on papyrus using reed pens. The papyrus was made from reeds, which grew along the edge of the River Nile. Papyrus was expensive, so for quick notes or handwriting practice, Egyptians used a flat stone or a broken piece of pot, now called an 'ostracon'. Only a few people could read and write in ancient Egypt. These were mainly scribes, who usually worked at the royal palaces or in the temples. When the last temple dedicated to the ancient Egyptian gods and goddess was closed in the fifth century AD, the skill of reading and writing hieroglyphs was lost.

ABOVE *The Rosetta Stone was a valuable tool for understanding ancient Egyptian hieroglyphs because it is inscribed with the same piece of writing in hieroglyphic, Demotic and Greek. Using the Greek, which could be read and understood, it was possible to start working out how to read hieroglyphs.*

ABOVE
This scribe's palette is made from wood with holes for two blocks of black and red ink and a slot for reed pens. The black ink was used for the main writing and the red ink was used to indicate important words or phrases and the beginning and end of particular parts of the text.

RIGHT *This painting from an ancient tomb shows geese being counted. The scribe standing on the far left has a writing palette tucked under his arm and holds a papyrus scroll.*

LEARNING

THE ANCIENT EGYPTIANS were skilled at measuring and surveying. These were skills which they needed to measure the annual flood of the River Nile and for their great building projects, such as the pyramids. Imhotep, who was in charge of the building of king Djoser's Step Pyramid at Saqqara around 2650 BC, was one of the first known architects. The ancient Egyptians were more interested in the practical use of mathematics than in theory. They worked out problems using a series of small calculations. Such calculations helped them to build large monuments and keep business records.

The world's earliest known doctor was an ancient Egyptian called Hesyra. He was doctor and dentist to king Djoser, in the 27th century BC. The ancient Egyptians wrote down their ideas about medicine, mathematics and astronomy on papyrus scrolls. They also wrote stories (including adventure stories), historical accounts, religious texts, poems and moral tales. Under Ptolemy I (who reigned from 305 to 285 BC), the city of Alexandria in northern Egypt became a centre of learning. Ptolemy had a famous library built in the city in 290 BC. The library was destroyed by fire in the third century AD.

ABOVE *A 'king list' of the different pharaohs who ruled Egypt.*

ABOVE *The Rhind Mathematical Papyrus is covered with thousands of calculations.*

ABOVE *This ostracon has lines from an Egyptian poem written on it in hieratic. The poem, known as the Tale of Sinuhe, tells the adventures of an ancient Egyptian called Sinuhe.*

ABOVE *Ptolemy I (reigned 305–285 BC).*

ABOVE *A clay model of an ancient Egyptian house. The house has stairs leading to the roof and there is an open courtyard, surrounded by a wall, in front of the house.*

■ BUILDINGS

MOST EVERYDAY BUILDINGS in ancient Egypt, such as houses and workshops, were built from mud brick. These bricks were made from a mixture of damp mud and straw, shaped in a wooden mould and then dried in the sun. Royal palaces were built from stone quarried from the ground. Official buildings and temples were mostly built of mud brick with some stone used for the doorways and columns. Some stone buildings and tombs were carved directly into tall stone cliffs. The ancient Egyptians built many temples for their gods. The central room of a temple, called the shrine, contained a statue of the god or goddess to whom the temple was dedicated. The shrine was surrounded by grand halls and courtyards. The entrance to the temple was marked by tall stone obelisks. Temples were decorated with pictures carved directly into the stone walls and columns, together with free-standing stone statues of pharaohs and gods.

ABOVE *The Valley of the Kings contains the tombs of kings from the 18th to 20th dynasties, including the tomb of Tutankhamun. The tombs were cut into the rocky cliffs on either side of the valley.*

ABOVE *Deir el-Medina was the village for the workers who built the royal tombs in the Valley of the Kings. It has over 120 houses for the workers and their families.*

Most of the pyramids in ancient Egypt were built during the Old Kingdom. Altogether more than 80 pyramids were built on the west side of the River Nile. The first pyramid was built for king Djoser, at Saqqara, in about 2650 BC. Each pyramid was the burial place of a king or a member of the royal family. A pyramid took a very long time to build, so work started while the king was still alive. Later on, kings were often buried in tombs cut into rock cliffs in places such as the Valley of the Kings and the Valley of the Queens.

BELOW *Rameses II built two temples at Abu Simbel. The temples were cut into the sandstone cliffs on the west bank of the River Nile. In front of the Great Temple are four colossal seated statues of the king, about 21 m (69 ft) high. Smaller figures of members of the royal family are carved next to the legs of each seated statue.*

EGYPT

THE PYRAMIDS AT GIZA

GIZA IS NEAR to Memphis, the first capital city of ancient Egypt. There are ten pyramids altogether at Giza. The three largest pyramids were built as the burial places for three ancient kings with seven smaller pyramids for members of the royal family. The largest pyramid at Giza is known as the Great Pyramid. It is 147 metres (482 ft) high. The Great Pyramid was built about 2570 BC for king Khufu. Inside are passages, shafts and chambers, including the King's Chamber, lined with red granite, which is where Khufu was probably buried. When it was first built, the outside of the pyramid was covered with a layer of smooth, white limestone. There were many smaller buildings around the Great Pyramid. One of these buildings was a mortuary temple, where offerings of food and prayers were made to the dead king. Several large boats were buried next to the pyramid for the king to use on his journey to the afterlife. The two other large pyramids at Giza were built for king Khafra and king Menkaure. There are three smaller pyramids next to king Menkaure's pyramid, one of which is the pyramid built for queen Khamerernebty.

ABOVE *This block of granite is carved with the name of the king Khufu.*

LEFT *Katep was a priest who worked at one of the temples near the pyramid of Khufu at Giza. In this statue he is shown with his wife Hetepheres.*

ABOVE *The Great Sphinx at Giza.*

THE GREAT SPHINX

THE GREAT SPHINX at Giza has the body of a lion and the head of a human. At its highest point it is 20 metres (66 ft) tall and it is 73 metres (240 ft) long. The Great Sphinx is carved from a natural outcrop of limestone. The face of the Sphinx is probably that of king Khafra (2558–2532 BC). Khafra had a pyramid at Giza and the Great Sphinx may have been made to guard his pyramid. The Great Sphinx was soon covered up by drifting sand from the surrounding desert. Around 1400 BC, Thutmose IV tried to clear the sand away. He carved an inscription on the Sphinx to record his efforts. The Great Sphinx was finally uncovered in AD 1925.

RIGHT *This is a piece of the Great Sphinx's beard. It was probably added about 1000 years after the Sphinx was originally carved. It later fell off and pieces were found in the sand beneath the Sphinx's head.*

LEFT *These sphinxes line the processional way between the temple of Amun at Karnak and Luxor temple.*

ABOVE *The pyramids at Giza. The white limestone which originally covered the outside of all the pyramids can still be seen at the top of the large pyramid in the middle.*

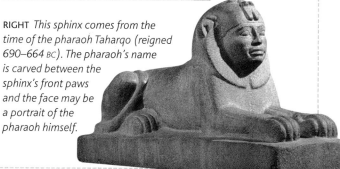

RIGHT *This sphinx comes from the time of the pharaoh Taharqo (reigned 690–664 BC). The pharaoh's name is carved between the sphinx's front paws and the face may be a portrait of the pharaoh himself.*

MUMMIFICATION

THE ANCIENT EGYPTIANS believed in an afterlife, where people would live forever in a land very similar to the Egypt they had lived in during their lifetime. They believed that it was necessary to take with them everything they needed for the afterlife when they were buried, including their body. The earliest Egyptian mummies were created naturally from bodies buried in the hot, dry desert sands. The hot sand slowly absorbed all the water from a body so that it was preserved. Later on, bodies were dried and preserved artificially using natron, a type of salt. After being dried, a body would be wrapped in linen bandages and placed in a coffin. The wrapped mummy, inside its coffin, would then be put in a tomb, together with enough belongings for the afterlife. The earliest known remains from an artificially dried mummy date from around 3000 BC. Only the most powerful and wealthy people in ancient Egypt were mummified, about one per cent of the total population. Mummification ended in the fourth century AD when Egypt became a Christian country.

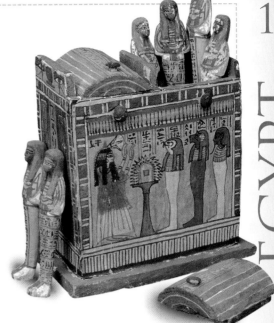

ABOVE *Shabti figures were placed in tombs to journey with the tomb owner to the afterlife. They were expected to work for the tomb owner. Some people had 401 shabtis in their tombs – one for each day of the year plus overseers to check that they were working hard. The shabtis were stored in a decorated wooden box.*

ABOVE *Henutmehyt was a priestess at one of the temples in ancient Thebes. This is the inner coffin for her mummified body and it is covered with a thin layer of gold.*

ABOVE *The ancient Egyptians believed that you needed to take your belongings with you to the afterlife. This wooden furniture was placed in a tomb for the tomb owner to use.*

RIGHT *This portrait dates from around AD 100, a time when Egypt was part of the Roman empire. The portrait was originally attached to the outside of a woman's coffin. The portrait was a way of remembering what the person looked like.*

LATER HISTORY

THE LAST RULER of an independent ancient Egypt was queen Cleopatra VII. After she died in 30 BC, Egypt became part of the Roman empire. When the Roman empire was divided into two smaller empires in AD 395, Egypt became part of the eastern Roman empire, later known as the Byzantine empire. By AD 642, Egypt was governed by the Muslim Arabs as part of their Islamic empire. Later, Egypt was one of the countries which formed part of the Ottoman empire, ruled by the Ottoman Dynasty, who came from Anatolia (modern Turkey). In AD 1822, Egypt came under British control. It gained its independence in AD 1953, when it became a republic with its capital city at Cairo.

ABOVE *Cleopatra VII, who reigned from 51 to 30 BC.*

ABOVE *In ancient Egyptian times, different pharaohs chose different cities to be the capital city of Egypt. Cairo is the capital city of the modern Republic of Egypt.*

GREECE

FROM AROUND 6500 BC, early farmers settled in small villages scattered across the ancient Greek landscape. About 2000 BC, large, organized societies appeared on the island of Crete. Life on Crete was based around a number of palaces which controlled the surrounding land and traded with places such as Mesopotamia and Egypt. The largest palace was at Knossos, in northern Crete. However, by 1450 BC, many of the Cretan palaces were no longer being used.

From about 1500 BC, the Mycenaeans, who lived on the Peloponnese on the Greek mainland, were the most organized, powerful people in Greece. The Mycenaeans lived in hilltop cities protected by massive stone walls. Around 1200 BC, the Mycenaeans became less powerful. After this, Greece went through what is called a Dark Age, when the skill of writing was lost and the population decreased. It was not until about 800 BC that new cities started to emerge. From about 800 to 336 BC cities such as Athens, Sparta and Corinth flourished and Greek people settled all around the coast of the Mediterranean Sea.

ABOVE *The Greeks traded their pottery all around the Mediterranean Sea. This Mycenaean bowl was found on the island of Cyprus. The vase is decorated with pictures of people riding in chariots pulled by horses.*

LEFT *Map of ancient Greece.*

BELOW *A bronze figure of a horse from the city-state of Sparta. The city was well known for its bronze figures.*

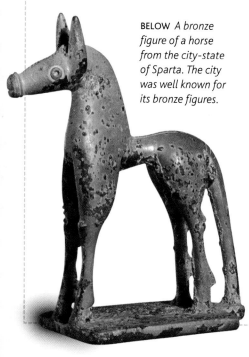

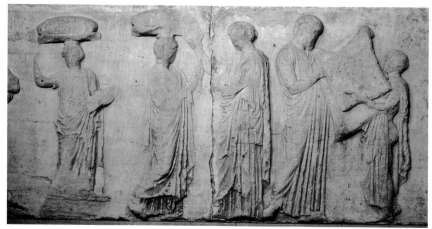

ABOVE *The people of ancient Athens believed that the goddess Athena protected their city. This sculpture from the Parthenon shows part of a festival held in honour of Athena.*

RULERS

From about 2000 BC, different areas on the island of Crete were controlled by one of the island's palaces. Each palace was in charge of the surrounding farmland and was probably run by a local ruler or possibly a religious leader. The palaces were centres for the collection and redistribution of produce from local farmers. To help with this, scribes worked at the palaces, recording what was being moved in and out. The Mycenaean fortified settlements on the Greek mainland were each ruled by a local ruler. Each ruler lived in a palace built inside the settlement's walls. Most other people lived outside the walls, including the traders who helped to make the Mycenaean rulers wealthy. This idea of an individual city being controlled by its own ruler continued when cities such as Athens, Sparta and Corinth developed from about 800 BC. Each city controlled the land around it and had its own ruler, army, laws and coins. A city could be ruled by a king, a small group of powerful people or an assembly of many people. In the city of Athens, an assembly of Athenian citizens met in the city's agora (market place) to discuss what should happen in the city. There were usually about 6,000 citizens present at an assembly meeting. Several smaller groups of citizens were elected annually to take important decisions, particularly about the defence of the city. This system was called democracy. In contrast, the city of Sparta was ruled by a king who made decisions with the help of advisers. In other cities a few powerful people or a powerful family might be in charge. During the sixth century BC, members of the Bacchiadae family ruled the city of Corinth. Sometimes the Greek cities joined together to form leagues. The cities in a league worked together to control the area of Greece around their cities. In 338 BC, the Macedonian king Philip II invaded Greece and for the first time ancient Greece was ruled by one person.

ABOVE *Pericles (c.495–429 BC) was re-elected to lead Athens nearly every year from 461 BC until his death in 429 BC. He introduced many new laws and supervised the rebuilding of Athens after the Persian Wars, including the building of the Parthenon on the Acropolis.*

ABOVE *This gold mask was buried with one of the rulers in the shaft graves at Mycenae.*

ABOVE *The assembly of Athenian citizens met here in the city's agora (market place).*

WRITING

ABOVE *The writing on this coin tells us that the coin was made in the Greek city of Syracuse on the island of Sicily.*

THE EARLIEST FORM of Greek writing developed on Crete. It used simple picture symbols. Around 1900 BC, these picture symbols were replaced by symbols which represented syllables. Today, this form of writing is known as Linear A. The Mycenaeans later developed a similar type of writing known as Linear B. This writing was used at the Cretan and Mycenaean palaces to record food supplies, animals and raw materials, such as wool, being brought to the palaces from the surrounding farmland. During the Greek Dark Age (from c.1100 to 800 BC), the skill of writing was lost. The Greek writing which developed around 800 BC used individual letters. Each letter represented a sound. These letters were based on the alphabet used by the Phoenicians. The Phoenicians used only consonants, to which the Greeks added vowels. At first, Greek was written from right to left. Then from the sixth century BC, Greek began to be written from left to right. The Greeks used writing to record laws for the people living in the different Greek cities. They also wrote plays and poems, recorded their ideas about science and mathematics, and conducted business in writing. The Greeks wrote on papyrus or parchment, which was rolled into a scroll. For quick notes, they wrote on wooden tablets covered with a layer of wax. To write on the wax, they used the pointed end of a bone or metal stylus. The flat end of the stylus could be used to smooth the wax flat again.

ABOVE *These tablets come from the palace at Knossos. The writing is a form of early Greek known as Linear B. This type of tablet was used to record goods and people passing through a palace.*

ABOVE AND LEFT *This Greek vase shows a scene from a Greek myth. The name of each Greek god or goddess shown on the vase is written beside the figure. The artist who painted the vase has signed his work with the words: 'Sophilos painted me'.*

LEARNING

THE GREEKS WERE influenced by ideas from Egypt and Babylon. In science, the Greeks thought of new ways to explain how the natural world and the human body worked. Greek doctors looked at the causes of diseases and tried to find out how to cure them. On the Greek island of Kos, Hippocrates (c.460 to 377 BC) started a medical school to teach people how to treat all kinds of diseases. The philosopher Aristotle (c.384 to 322 BC) opened a school in Athens as a place for people to learn and also to think about how the world worked and the purpose of life. One of his interests was the natural world, and he devised a system which organized all living animals and plants into groups. The Greeks were interested in recording not only when events happened, but also why they happened. Herodotus (c.484 to 420 BC) wrote a history text which tried both to record and to explain past events in Greek history. Greek playwrights wrote both tragic and comic plays. The playwright Aeschylus (c.525 to 456 BC) wrote over 90 plays. The Greeks also wrote poetry. The poet Sappho (c.620 to 580 BC) was famous for her nine books of lyrical poetry.

ABOVE *Socrates (c. 469-399 BC) was an ancient Greek philosopher. He tried to find out the nature of knowledge itself by asking questions and by discussion.*

LEFT *This Greek vase shows a scene from the Odyssey. It illustrates the episode in which Odysseus and his companions have to sail past the Sirens.*

ABOVE *Homer is believed to be the author of the epic poems the Iliad and the Odyssey. No portraits of Homer were made when he was alive (around 700 BC). This marble portrait was created in the second century BC for the ancient royal library at Pergamon.*

■ BUILDINGS

A CRETAN PALACE functioned both as the religious centre and the trade centre for the surrounding area. Each palace contained hundreds of small rooms, courtyards, staircases, storage rooms, workshops, religious shrines and a 'grand room' used by the ruler. The palace walls were covered in beautiful paintings of nature scenes with plants and animals, and of ceremonial scenes with people. Around each palace was a town with houses. In the countryside surrounding the palace were small settlements and individual farmsteads. Most buildings on Crete were built of mud brick, wood or stone.

The Mycenaeans built their settlements on hilltops on the Greek mainland. These settlements were surrounded by massive stone walls. Inside the walls were a palace, houses, shrines and workshops. Farmers lived outside the walls, farming the nearby land.

After 800 BC, a number of cities, such as Athens, Corinth and Sparta, emerged across Greece. The centre of each city was the agora (market place). The agora was surrounded by the city's temples, law courts and shops. Important city buildings were built of stone. These buildings were decorated with tall columns and stone sculptures. Houses were made of mud brick and wood with clay-tile roofs, and they were usually built around an open courtyard.

ABOVE *A Mycenaean hill settlement.*

ABOVE *This wall painting from the palace at Knossos, on Crete, shows a marine scene with dolphins and fish.*

RIGHT *The Parthenon was built on the Acropolis in Athens between 447 and 432 BC, in honour of the goddess Athena. The Parthenon was decorated with sculptures. Inside the temple, there was a tall statue of the goddess together with a treasury which contained all the gifts given to Athena.*

THE OLYMPIC GAMES

MANY SPORTING festivals were held throughout ancient Greece to honour the gods and goddesses. The largest of these events, the Olympic Games, was a festival of sports in honour of the god Zeus, held at Olympia. According to tradition, the first Olympic Games were held in 776 BC. Soon athletes and spectators were travelling from all over Greece to take part. To make sure that everybody could travel in safety to and from the Olympic Games, a truce was called between all Greek city-states while the Games were taking place.

The ancient Greek Olympics took place every four years during August and lasted for several days. The Games were organized by the nearby city of Elis. Events included horse racing, chariot racing, boxing, sprinting and the pentathlon (discus and javelin throwing, jumping, wrestling and running). There were no team sports. On the last day, the winners were awarded olive wreaths made from a sacred olive tree which grew at Olympia. For the ancient Greeks, the Olympic Games were an important religious festival. As well as the sports events, there was also a procession and a banquet.

The Olympic Games held in honour of Zeus was a sporting competition for male athletes. Female athletes took part in a festival at Olympia called the Heraia, in honour of the goddess Hera, at which they competed in running races. The ancient Olympic Games probably ended in AD 391, when the Roman emperor Theodosius I abolished the worship of pagan gods.

LEFT *There were several running races held during the ancient Olympic Games. The longest race was about 5 km (3 miles) long. The shortest race was a sprint over a distance of about 190 m (208 yards).*

RIGHT *These are the stone slabs used to mark the starting line for the running races at Olympia. All the runners had to line up with their toes on the grooves in the stones.*

ABOVE *These athletes are taking part in a long jump competition. They hold weights made from metal or stone in each hand, which they swung at their sides to help them to jump further. The sticks in the ground show how far the other competitors have already jumped.*

ABOVE *This bronze figure of a female runner comes from Sparta. Women athletes took part in sporting events held in honour of the ancient Greek goddesses.*

COINS

COINS WERE used in the kingdom of Lydia (in what is now western Turkey) from the seventh century BC. Coins were a useful standard unit of payment and their use quickly spread from Lydia to nearby Greece. The first Greek coins were made from electrum, a natural mixture of gold and silver. The coins were stamped with a design to show where they had been made. In the middle of the sixth century BC, one of the first Greek cities to issue coins was Corinth. Coins from Corinth were stamped with a picture of Pegasus, the winged horse, which was the city's symbol. For the first 200 years of their use, Greek coins were made from precious metals, such as electrum, silver and gold. The city of Athens controlled the silver mines at Laurion, so they made most of their coins from silver. Later, in the fifth century BC some Greek coins started to be made from bronze. Greek coins were used all around the Mediterranean area and their use spread to other countries.

ABOVE *This coin comes from Lydia and was made about 650 BC. It is made from electrum.*

RIGHT *Some Greek coins carry a picture connected to the name of the city where they were made. This coin has a picture of a seal. The ancient Greek word for seal is 'phoce' and this coin may therefore have come from the Greek city of Phocaea.*

ABOVE *This silver coin was made in ancient Athens. It has a picture of Athena, the city's patron goddess, on one side and an owl, one of Athena's symbols, on the other side.*

LATER HISTORY

IN 338 BC, Greece came under the rule of the Macedonian king Philip II. Philip's son, Alexander, went on to build a huge empire which included Greece, Persia, Egypt and much of western Asia. However, after Alexander's death in 323 BC, Macedonian control over Greece became weaker and groups of cities joined together to rule their own regions. In 168 BC, the Romans conquered Macedonia. Then, in 146 BC, they invaded Greece and it became part of the Roman empire. During the fourth century AD, the Roman empire was divided into two smaller empires. Greece was in the eastern empire, later known as the Byzantine empire. When the Byzantine empire fell to the Ottoman Turks in AD 1483, Greece became part of their Ottoman empire. In AD 1821, a Greek state, based around the Peloponnese on the Greek mainland, gained independence from the Ottoman empire. By AD 1913, Crete and northern Greece had also become part of the modern country of Greece. Today, Greece is a republic with Athens as its capital city.

LEFT *The Roman emperor Hadrian travelled all around the Roman empire during his reign (AD 117-138). When visiting Greece, he took part in religious and cultural events.*

RIGHT *The Macedonian king Alexander created a vast empire that stretched from Greece to the River Ganges in India. He died in the city of Babylon in 323 BC.*

LEFT *Athens is the capital city of modern Greece. At the centre of the city is the Acropolis on which stands the Parthenon.*

ROME

ABOVE *The first forum to be built in Rome was in a valley between the Capitoline and Palatine hills. The forum was the political, economic and religious centre of early Rome.*

THE CITY OF ROME began as a group of small settlements on the hills near the River Tiber. The people who lived in these villages were farmers who settled the area between 2000 and 1000 BC. One of the main trading routes across the Italian peninsula ran over a bridge built across the River Tiber near the villages. The villages grew wealthy from trade and during the eighth century BC joined together to become one town. This town was Rome. From 616 to 510 BC, Rome was ruled by the Etruscans. The Etruscans came from the region north of Rome, where they lived in a number of cities each ruled by its own king. Under its Etruscan kings, Rome grew into a city with a forum (market place), temples, stone houses, a palace and possibly a city wall. The last Etruscan king's reign ended in 510 BC, after which Rome became a republic ruled by an assembly of leading Roman citizens. The Romans gradually began to conquer and colonize the land around the city, and by 270 BC Rome controlled all of the Italian peninsula. Over the next 250 years, the Romans built up a vast empire. From 27 BC this empire was ruled by emperors. The Roman empire reached its greatest extent under the emperor Trajan (who reigned from AD 98 to 117) when the Romans controlled territory in Europe, Africa and Asia.

ABOVE *A pottery model of a simple village house, made around 850 BC. Houses like this were built using wooden posts with wattle and daub walls and a thatched roof.*

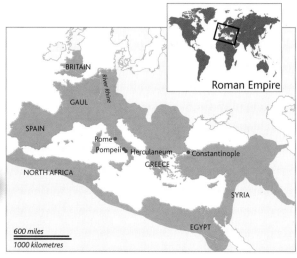

ABOVE *The Roman empire at its largest extent, about 120 AD.*

RIGHT *This wall painting shows Etruscan people. The Etruscans ruled the city of Rome for about 100 years from 616 BC.*

■ RULERS

THE EARLY ROMAN villages on the banks of the River Tiber were ruled by individual village leaders. It was not until the villages became one settlement that they had a single ruler. In the seventh century BC, the Etruscan Tarquin I (who reigned from 616 to 579 BC) took control of Rome and turned it into a city. Rome was ruled by members of the Tarquin family until 510 BC, when the last king lost his throne. After this, a Republic was set up to govern the city. Each year two consuls were elected to rule, advised by the Senate (a council of experienced politicians). From about 150 BC, as Rome and the land it controlled around the Mediterranean grew in both size and wealth, various powerful people tried to take control of the city of Rome. Then, in 45 BC, Julius Caesar successfully took over as sole ruler. He never called himself king or emperor though his great-nephew, Augustus, who ruled after him, became the first emperor of Rome. The Senate continued to give advice about how the empire should be run but it was now under the control of the emperor. When Augustus died in AD 14, he passed the title of emperor on to his adopted son, Tiberius. Rome was ruled by emperors for the next 400 years. The Roman empire was divided into provinces each of which was controlled by a Roman governor, who commanded the troops and was responsible for law and order. There was also a procurator for each province, who was in charge of collecting taxes and paying the army. Both officials were chosen by the emperor and had a staff of slaves and military clerks to help them with their work.

ABOVE *The emperor Hadrian (who reigned from AD 117 to 38). Hadrian ordered the building of a great wall across northern Britain, the northern boundary of his empire.*

ABOVE *Coins carried the image of the emperor across the empire. On this coin, Augustus (reigned 27 BC–AD 14) is shown as a strong ruler who has brought peace to the Roman Empire.*

ABOVE *Agrippina the Elder was a popular member of the imperial family. She was the grand-daughter of the emperor Augustus and mother of the emperor Caligula.*

ABOVE *Hadrian's Wall is 80 Roman miles long (117 km or 73 modern miles). It took six years to build.*

ABOVE *In this wall painting from Pompeii, the woman holds a stylus and wax writing tablet and the man holds a papyrus scroll.*

WRITING

MANY DIFFERENT LANGUAGES were spoken across the Roman empire though only a few were used for writing. In the west of the empire (in places such as Spain, Gaul and Britain), Latin was used for official documents, trade and conducting government, while in the east (in places such as Egypt, Syria and Greece) Greek was used for the same purposes. The Romans used simple symbols for their numbers: I for 1, V for 5, X for 10, C for 100 and M for 1000. These symbols could be put together to make other numbers. The Romans wrote with split-nib pens, made of reed or metal. They wrote in ink on papyrus, wood and parchment. Quick notes and letters were often written with a metal stylus on a wax tablet, which could be smoothed over and re-used. More important documents were written on scrolls made from sheets of papyrus glued together to make a long strip, which was then rolled up around a wooden or ivory stick. Scrolls were written on in columns, so that as the scroll was unrolled, it could be read column by column. By the third century AD, books were being made from parchment cut into sheets, sewn together and bound in a cover. Rome, together with many other towns and cities, had public libraries.

ABOVE *An invitation to a birthday party sent by Claudia Severa to her friend Sulpicia Lepidina. The invitation is written on two thin pieces of wood that were folded and tied together. It was found at Vindolanda, a Roman fort in northern Britain.*

RIGHT *This wooden writing tablet was originally covered in a thin layer of wax.*

LEFT *Roman ink was made from soot mixed with water. The person who used this pottery ink-well was probably called Iucundus. His name has been scratched on the outside of the pot.*

LEARNING

THE ROMANS USED Latin to write down their ideas and creative thoughts. The architect Vitruvius (c. 70 BC to early first century AD) wrote about engineering, building techniques, materials and decoration in a book called *De Architectura* (*About Architecture*). The Romans were also interested in recording their history. For example, Tacitus (c. AD 56 to 120) wrote a detailed history of the Roman empire while Suetonius (c. AD 69 to mid-second century) wrote about the life and times of twelve of the Roman emperors from Julius Caesar to Domitian.

Roman plays were often based on Greek plays. Comedies were popular, and the Roman playwright Plautus (c.254 to184 BC) wrote over 130 comic plays. The Roman poet Ovid (43 BC to AD 17) wrote an epic poem in fifteen books called *Metamorphoses*, which is about people who change into animals and plants. Debating a point of view was considered an important skill in ancient Rome and both Cicero (106 to 43 BC) and Pliny the Younger (c. AD 62 to113) were well-known for their skill at speaking as well as for their written works.

ABOVE *Roman building skills are celebrated on this coin which shows the Colosseum in Rome. The coin was made in AD 80, the year in which the Colosseum was opened by the Roman emperor Titus.*

ABOVE *The Romans believed that creative thoughts were inspired by the Muses. This silver casket is decorated with figures which represent different creative activities such as poetry, dance and theatre.*

RIGHT *These two figures from the casket show the muse of music with an instrument (on the left) and the muse of the theatre with an actor's mask (on the right).*

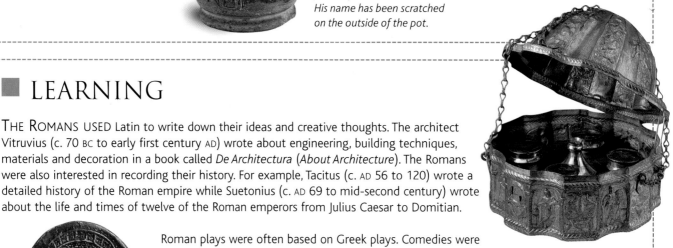